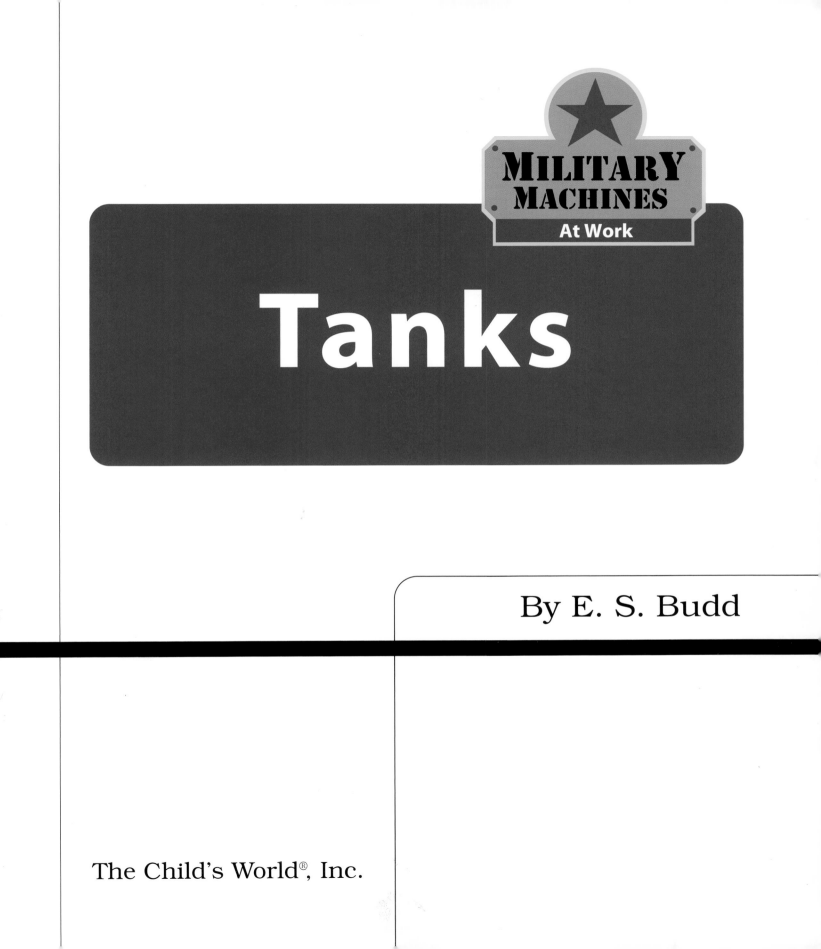

MILITARY MACHINES
At Work

Tanks

By E. S. Budd

The Child's World®, Inc.

Published by The Child's World®, Inc.
PO Box 326
Chanhassen, MN 55317-0326
800-599-READ
www.childsworld.com

Design and Production:
The Creative Spark, San Juan Capistrano, CA

Photos: © 2002 David M. Budd Photography
        Page 5 is courtesy of the United States Army.

We thank the personnel at Fort Carson (Colorado Springs, CO)
for their help and cooperation in preparing this book.

Library of Congress Cataloging-in-Publication Data

Budd, E. S.
Tanks / by E.S. Budd.
        p. cm.
ISBN 1-56766-984-0 (library bound)
1. Tanks (Military science)—Juvenile literature.
[1. Tanks (Military science)]   I. Title.
UG446.5 .B83 2001
623.7'4752—dc21
                                        2001000341

Contents

On the Job

On the job, tanks protect soldiers on the battlefield.

Tanks have **armor** made of very thick metal. The armor protects soldiers inside the tanks from gunfire.

Tanks move on **tracks.** The tracks help tanks travel over rough ground.

The **turret** is on top of the tank. It has a large gun. The turret can spin around to fire the gun in any direction.

There are two **hatches** on top of the turret. Soldiers enter the tank through the hatches. The hatches are closed during battle.

The turret has room for three soldiers. The commander tells the other soldiers what to do. The loader puts **ammunition** in the gun.

The third soldier is called the
gunner. He uses **controls** to aim
and fire the gun.

A tank's driver sits in a

different area.

The driver looks through **periscopes**

to see outside.

Climb Aboard!

Would you like to see where the driver sits? The tank has a special steering control. The driver uses other controls to move the tank. He enters the driver's area through another hatch.

Up Close

The inside

1. The controls

2. The driver's seat

The turret

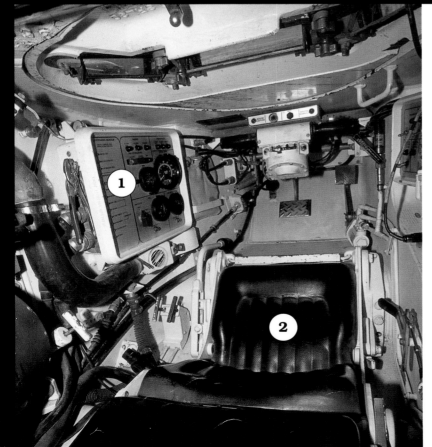

The driver's area

Outside

1. The tracks

2. The gun

3. The armor

4. The driver's area

5. The hatches

6. The periscopes

7. The turret

Glossary

ammunition (am-yeh-NISH-un)
Ammunition is something that can be fired from guns or other weapons. On a tank, a loader puts ammunition in the gun.

armor (AR-mur)
Armor is a covering made of metal or another strong material. A tank has armor made of thick metal to protect soldiers on the battlefield.

controls (kun-TROHLZ)
Controls are buttons, switches, and other tools that make a machine work. A tank driver uses controls to move the tank.

hatches (HATCH-ez)
Hatches are openings on the top of a tank or other vehicle. Soldiers enter a tank through hatches.

periscopes (PAYR-ih-skohpz)
Periscopes are tools that use mirrors to see outside of something. Soldiers inside a tank use periscopes to look outside.

tracks (TRAX)
Tracks are huge belts that run around and around to move a machine forward and backward. A tank moves on tracks.

turret (TUR-it)
A turret is the upper part of a tank. Three soldiers can sit in a tank's turret.